Time Passages

Yesterday is but today's memory,

and tomorrow is today's dream.

~ *Khalil Gibran*

Time Passages

Time Passages

paul Bluestein

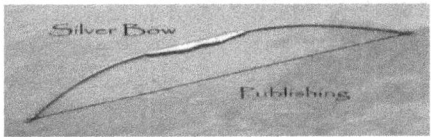

Silver Bow Publishing
720 Sixth Street, Box # 5
New Westminster, BC
CANADA   V3L3C5

Time Passages

Title: Time Passages
Author: paul Bluestein
Cover Art: "Silver Moon of the Violet Waters" painting by Candice James
Cover Design: Candice James
Layout and Editing: Candice James
ISBN: 9781774030851 (print)
ISBN: 9781774030868 (e-book)
© 2020 Silver Bow Publishing

All rights reserved including the right to reproduce or translate this book or any portions thereof, in any form except for the use of short passages for review purposes, no part of this book may be reproduced, in part or in whole, or transmitted in any form or by any means, electronically or mechanically, including photocopying, recording, or any information or storage retrieval system without prior permission in writing from the publisher or a license from the Canadian Copyright Collective Agency (Access Copyright).

Library and Archives Canada Cataloguing in Publication

Title: Time passages / Paul Bluestein.
Names: Bluestein, Paul, 1947- author.
Description: Poetry.
Identifiers: Canadiana (print) 2020017777X | Canadiana (ebook) 20200177818 | ISBN 9781774030851
    (softcover) | ISBN 9781774030868 (HTML)
Classification: LCC PS3602.L84 T56 2020 | DDC 813/.6—dc23Email:

info@silverbowpublishing.com
Website: www.silverbowpublishing.com

Acknowledgements

The following poems first appeared in:

"(Thanksgiving) Morning" *50wordstories, 2018*
"Waltz Time" *PenWorks, (Trumbull Arts Festival), 2018*
 "You Can Hear It Coming" *Remington Review, 2018*
"Hurricane Season" and "Moving Day" *Verse-Virtual, 2019*
"October Cathedral" *Young Ravens Literary Review*, 2019
"Autumn's Approach" *From The Edge Poetry Magazine, 2019*
"The Dogs Know" *The Weekly Avocet, 2018*
"Legacy" *Heron Tree, 2019*
"Winter Highway" *Boston Literary Magazine, 2020*
"Winter Blue", "Writing Dance" and "The Morning Crept Up" *Nine Muses Poetry, 2018*
"Waiting" *The Waco WordFest Anthology, 2019*
"Birdsong" and" The Last Page" *Remington Review, 2019*
"Hard Place" *Tigershark, 2018*
"4th of July" *Steam Ticket, 2019*
"Woodstock: August 15, 1969" *Pilcrow & Dagger, 2019*
"Sacred Space", "Recovery" and "Loose Change" *Penumbra, 2019*
"Before and After" *Foxglove Journal, 2018*
"Samarra" *The Literary Nest*, 2019
"City Boy" *Willawaw Journal, 2019*
"Constellations" *Nightingale & Sparrow, 2019*
"Confession" *Poetry Quarterly, 2018*
"Chris", "By(e) Chance" and "Kitchen Table" The *Drabble, 2018*
"Reverie" (as "In Dreams") *Snapdragon, 2019*
"Outgoing Tide" *Dragon Poet Review, 2019*
"Somewhere Up Ahead" *Black Poppy Review, 2019*
"Go Out and Play" *Pilcrow & Dagger, 2018*
"So Close to Home" *Vita Brevis, 2018*
"If I Had Known" *Linden Avenue Literary Journal, 2018*
"Last Leaf" *Canyon Voices, 2020*
"Old Man" *Third Wednesday, 2020*

Time Passages

Time Passages

Dedication

This first collection is dedicated to Lynda Shannon,
my wife, bridge partner and fashion advisor
whose support for this project I could not repay
even with a lifetime of coffee ice cream
with chocolate sprinkles.

Time Passages

Table of Contents

Autumn

(Thanksgiving) Morning ... 13
Waltz Time ... 14
You Can Hear It Coming ... 16
Hurricane Season ... 17
October Cathedral ... 18
Autumn's Approach ... 19
The Dogs Know ... 20

Winter

Legacy ... 23
Winter Highway ... 24
Winter Blue ... 25
Waiting ... 26
Birdsong ... 27
Winter Ballet ... 28

Spring

Hard Place ... 31
Exodus ... 32
ReNew ... 33
Dandelions ... 34

Summer

Are We There? ... 37
4th of July ... 38
Woodstock: August 15, 1969 ... 39

Time Passages

Romance ... 43
Anniversary ... 44
Sacred Space ... 45
Allspice Goes Next to the Anise ... 46
Recovery ... 47
Moving Day ... 48
The Last Page ... 49
The Appointment in Samarra ... 50
Before and After ... 51
Samarra ... 52
Caught in Between ... 53
City Boy ... 54
A Small Sidewalk Café ... 55
Creation ... 56
Constellations ... 57
Silence ... 58
Confession ... 59
Just Close the Door ... 60
Chris ... 61
Loose Change ... 62
Edge of Love ... 63
Reverie ... 64
Outgoing Tide ... 65
Writing Dance ... 66
The Morning Crept Up ... 67
Sabbath ... 68
Somewhere Up Ahead ... 69
By(e) Chance ... 70
Downsized ... 71
Kitchen Table ... 72
Go Out and Play ... 73
So Close to Home ... 74
If I Had Known ... 75
Last Leaf ... 76
Old Man ...77

Time Passages

Autumn

Time Passages

(Thanksgiving) Morning

I bark ... and the sun comes up.
Morning.
He fetches his coffee, my biscuit.
Toast and a treat.
He'll read the newspaper;
I'll dream of slow, inattentive cats.

When he reaches down to ruffle my fur,
his hand feels like the afternoon sun.

This must be what he calls Thanksgiving.

Time Passages

Waltz Time

The afternoon beach is not deserted --
that solitude the gulls and waves
will not find for another month or so.

Small children sit on lifeguard stands
while mothers squint into the setting sun,
pretending it is still July.

As I walk, I count my steps:

One...two...three
One...two...three
One...two...three

Strides in the 3/4 rhythm of the "R" months
that have just begun:

Sep...*tem*...ber
Oct...*to*...ber
No...*vem*...ber

I walk past horseshoe crabs
imprisoned by circles in the sand,
drawn by innocent hands
that don't yet know sand-circles
are nearly at an end.

As I reach the rise of the jetty
and turn to see the sweep of sand
and sea and setting sun,
running children turn their backs on chasing waves
as surely as the calendar pages
have turned their backs on summer,
abandoning August for the rhythm of autumn.

Time Passages

Soon we will dance
to the waltz of falling leaves,
Slowing, slowing ...
until we come to the frozen measures of winter.

You Can Hear It Coming

Autumn, a passing thought just weeks ago,
now surrounds the days.

Birds frantically prepare for their journey,
flying off to places you have read about
but have never seen.
I hear them call out,
urging one another to hurry
as the cicadas' song rises and falls in the late afternoon,
like waves breaking on September's shore.

The trees lean toward one another
and whisper about the colors they will wear
while their leaves shimmy in the freshening air,
sounding like the swish
of the sheets of Halloween ghosts
that will soon haunt October streets.

Wind chimes that were silent in the summer stillness
come to life like church bells
that suddenly awaken to find it is Sunday.

The distant music of ice cream trucks
and the splashing of garden hoses is fading,
replaced by the sound of wood being split and stacked.

Close your eyes and listen.
You can hear fall coming.

Hurricane Season

Dogs shelter under the porch
and the birds fall silent.
The choir of wind chimes waits quietly,
until the rising wind rolls in like waves
breaking on a leafy shore,
building into a tsunami roar.
Then, metallic voices puncture the air,
a dissonant chorale
conducted by the wildly waving arms of nearby trees.

Red traffic lights and red taillights
flash neon-bright against the darkening sky,
while worried eyes watch somber gray clouds
gather in the south like Confederate battalions.
Soon, the streets will be surrendered
to an advancing army of blowing newspapers
and early autumn leaves.

Overhead, a solitary gull
flies on the wings of the storm.
Cameron is coming.

October Cathedral

We stand at the threshold of October's cathedral,
one of the dozen calendared sanctuaries
built within each cycle of the moon.
Stained-glass windows of crayon-color leaves
and a vaulted dome of blue sky.
The sun is snared by the hands of the autumn clock
and pulled down from the afternoon sky too soon.
All of nature is slowly turning away from summer,
but, as lovers often do,
looking back one last time before leaving.

Autumn's Approach [An American Cinquain]

Music
of wind chimes drifts
through the September night,
a breezy summer coda. Then,
silence.

The Dogs Know

My dogs know before I do.
Maybe it is the changing light, cooling nights
or the rustle of the cicadas.
Or, maybe they can feel the world
straining at the leash held by the sun.

While I wonder at clouds overhead,
they keep their noses to the ground
and investigate mysteries
buried beneath the roots of oaks.
They revel in the morning as if they know
the day will soon be short-shanked by October.
They chase chittering squirrels
with the energy of forty-thousand years of instinct,
then return slowly,
like children leaving the playground.

I watch the calendar, but they live in the moment,
and they know, before I do, that autumn is coming.

Time Passages

Winter

Time Passages

Legacy

I will not see summer again,

so I walk the winter shoreline
and take from December's days what I can.

The dogs run ahead, snarling and snapping,
playing the wolf-games taught to them by ancestors
that lie sleeping just beneath their skins.

The waves come and go in an ancient rhythm,
a cymbal crash and snare tattoo,
played for a million years
before I stepped onto this snow-frosted sand.

I walk the low tide at a slow pace,
down to the stone pier
where, under an August sun,
I would have sat to watch the resolve of the rocks
worn away by the patience of the sea.
But it is too late in a short day to linger,
and before the waves can smooth the sand,
I follow my footsteps back
to where I began.

Winter Highway

The eastern sun shines
through a tattered blanket of clouds
thrown carelessly on the bed of the sky.
I drive north and the shadow of my car
stretches into the oncoming traffic. A ghost car,
speeding in the wrong lane,
colliding with southbound cars,
but the only sound is the wind and the miles
rolling away beneath my wheels.
The hills, rising up in the west,
have shed their leaf-soft June fur
and grown a spiky coat of bare trees
whose leaves now lie
dead and brown beside the highway,
victims of their own collision
with immovable December.

Winter Blue

Winter blue,
December sun just leaves me cold.
No promise that the New Year holds
can warm me while I'm still so far from you
and feeling winter blue.

The moonlight silhouettes the trees,
the moon sails through a cloudy sea.
It looks like maybe it will snow tonight
and change these winter blues to winter white.

Winter days are trickling by;
I stop at Al's and have a drink ...
or two.

I sit and watch the falling snow.
The music on the radio
can't make me feel the way I used to,
sounding out of tune and winter blue.

The snowfall covers up the town.
It steals the color and the sound
and if I get the wish I wish tonight,
I'll pack my bags and catch the midnight flight.

Waiting

Water, climbing down the rocky hills,
is arrested in its attempted escape
and imprisoned in the lock-up of December.

Trees stretch out their winter arms,
now clothed in long-sleeved snow,
trying to catch the early-falling sun
that slips through gnarled fingers.
All of nature has gone silent ...

In that stillness, I remember August sun
rising red-orange over a Midwest cornfield.
The alarm-clock buzz of cicadas
and the rustling cornstalks
wake me from my sleeping-porch bed
and my ten-year-old feet
take me to the blue-brown river where
water-worn stones sleep.

The current of minutes and months
that swirls around me now
will never take me back
to that childhood summer.
But spring will come,
the iron cell door of winter will open,
and there will be a new beginning.

Birdsong

In the early winter morning,
drinking coffee by the window,
glass etched by the overnight frost,
I heard a chickadee singing.
Just two notes,
brief as a firefly's flash,
but long enough to echo
throughout a December day.

Winter Ballet

Midnight comes and goes while I wait
for the snow that was promised by 2:00 a.m.
I stare out at the dark stage of the night,
lit by the ghost-light of the walkway,
watching for the first snowflake to fall -
a prima ballerina
pirouetting through the icy air.
I can hear the orchestral wind tuning,
its snarling and moaning
muted by panes of frosted glass,
accompanied by the clank
and hiss of the basement boiler.
The storm arrives like a ticker tape parade -
confetti drifting down,
dressing the city in satin,
hiding the loneliness behind
a wall of winter white.

Time Passages

Spring

Time Passages

Hard Place

My home is a hard place,
with towns that come by their names honestly:
Rocky Hill.
Stonington.
Black Rock.

The hard rain of a Nor'easter
and the hard freeze of winter
suits people whose grandfathers built walls from rock
that grew in every field and hillside.
Hard people whose faces and lives
are carved by the chisel of steady habits.

But when May comes
and the memory of March is gone,
hearts hardened by the granite-gray winter
surrender to the sun.

Exodus

Before the crocuses
poke their purple fingers up out of the ground,
before the forsythia and daffodils
splash the landscape yellow,
the clock springs ahead
and we are plunged into daylight.

From the winter that kept us in bondage,
prisoners in our homes and coats,
slaves to boots and gloves, hats and scarves,
we escape.

Led by the sun and the promise of summer,
we are free.

Re-New

The distant hills have grown soft, green fur.
The air which, just a month ago, barked
and bit my ankles, now licks my face
with a warm and gentle tongue.
The daylight comes earlier
and stays longer, but still leaves
before its welcome is worn out.
It invites my winter self to look at the world
with warmer eyes. To notice
plumes of yellow forsythia,
spumes of grass and women in red dresses.
A time to be new again.

Dandelions

I see the summer gardeners
tending carefully nurtured lawns,
and contemplate digging out
the dandelions that have grown
among the flowers of my life.
Weeds of past regrets.
Deeds not done, words unsaid,
sins of careless omission.

But digging there,
among roots that grow deep in the soul,
is difficult and dangerous work.
Who knows what might be unearthed?

I've earned every line on my face,
and the right to sit quietly in the sun
looking out over my garden,
littered here and there with dandelions
which will, in time, turn gray,
die and be carried away by the wind.

Time Passages

Summer

Time Passages

Are We There?

January,
February,
March.
Are we there yet?

Like children on the way to grandmother's house,
we look forward to being spoiled for just one day.
The longest day.
The solstice, where summer begins.

We ask, "Are we there yet?"
and the calendar answers "Almost".

April.
May.
June.

Be quiet now.
Listen to the road
and watch the clouds as they roll across the sky
like tumbleweeds across the desert floor.
Enjoy the trip.
We'll be there before you know it.

Under the spell
of the long light of summer,
we forget that unseen,
behind a curtain of August leaves,
the evergreens wait patiently for December.

4th of July

I stand in the stifling abandoned theater,
where my parents once sat while Dorothy
skipped down the yellow-brick road toward Oz.
There in the balcony, I can see my father
who would march down a snow-covered road to Bastogne
and no matter how many times he clicked his heels,
he would not come home again.

In the empty seats, I hear
the neighbor's sons
who shared my hopes and high school classes,
algebra and Spanish grammar,
their names inscribed on diplomas
and later, on black marble.

The dim and distant theater of childhood
now hosts only an audience of spiders
spinning webs that catch the flickering dreams
of days past and promises unfulfilled.
Outside, the flags hang lifeless,
honor and old glories
melting in the hammering heat;
not the sigh of a breeze or hope.

Woodstock: August 15, 1969

(Found poem comprised of the titles of songs played on the first day of the Woodstock Music & Art Fair)

Snow White Lady
She's Gone
A Note That Read
I Can't Make It Anymore

Swing Low, Sweet Chariot
Take Me Back To the Sweet Sunny South
I'm a Stranger Here
We Shall Overcome

How Can We Hang Onto a Dream?
One Day At a Time
Sweet Sir Galahad

Smile, Handsome Johnny
High Flying Bird
I Wondered Where You'd Be

Misty Roses, Hickory Wind,
Close To It All
And When It's Over
From the Prison

I Shall Be Released
No Expectations
Simple Song of Freedom

Why Oh Why
America, What's Wrong
Beautiful People
You Upset the Grace of Living When You Lie.

Time Passages

Time Passages

Time Passages

Romance

"Introvert?"
    "Extrovert!"
"Jazz?"
    "Disco."
"Cats?"
    "Dogs."
"Chocolate"?
    "My favorite!"
"I'm not really looking for a relationship"
she said.
"Neither am I",
I lied.

We were perfect for one another.

Her mother attended the wedding dressed in black.
My mother just pursed her lips and shook her head.
They were certain it wouldn't last six months.

They've been wrong for thirty-eight years.

Anniversary

Close your book, turn the light out.
Do you remember the way
we would talk until daybreak?
Wasn't that just yesterday?

Close your eyes, lay your head down;
let the day slip away.
I will love you tomorrow
like I love you today.

You've learned to read me like a book -
every word, every look.

We are shells on the shoreline,
stranded here on the sand,
washed by waves that make changes
to the lives we had planned.

There are still miles to travel,
many bridges to cross,
many roads to unravel
many ways to be lost.

I may not remember
all the whys and wheres and whens,
but I know that I love you
now as I did then.

Standing here at the threshold
autumn grass turning brown,
looking back at a lifetime
nothing's lost that can't be found.

Sacred Space

Between dreamless sleep
and the insistent intrusion
of the clamor of the day,
there is a sacred space -
a time of deep quiet,
a time for being still
and waiting patiently
for better angels to appear.
To not be seduced by the ticking clock
or servant to the demands of an hour.

Watch how the rising sun is broken
by the imperfections of your windows
into rainbows on the sunlit floor,
and accept that the whole world can be contained
in the coffee cup you hold in your hands.

Allspice Goes Next to the Anise

The doctor said "get a pencil,
and something to write on."
Suddenly, the phone was a snake in my hand,
rattling and ready to strike.

        The Allspice goes next to the Anise.
           Basil next to the Bay Leaf.
      Throw out the Berbere I never tried.

"I'm sorry.
The biopsy was positive.
Cancer."

        Cinnamon, Cloves,
        Cumin, then Dill.

"You'll need surgery.
Probably radiation...
possibly chemotherapy."

        Mace beside the Marjoram.
        Rosemary, Sage,
        Tarragon and Thyme.
        Never enough Thyme.

        Sometimes, all you can do
        is reorganize the spice rack.

Recovery

The surgeons, who had their knife-fight
with the cancer while you slept,
provide pain-relievers and platitudes.
Acquaintances and colleagues send white light,
flowers and advice.
Friends bring food and books to read
and listen while you tell your story.
The children visit, armed with
pictures of grand-children and
family lore that begins "Remember when?"
The web connects you to other women,
some cured, others hopeful,
none hopeless.
Even the daily news is delivered to the door.
What is there for me to do
other than sit by your side
and silently hold your hand?

Moving Day

The eighteen-wheeler,
bright as a Barnum & Bailey trailer,
arrives in the gray morning mist
of a cold, January Monday.
The house is as empty as we feel,
nothing remaining except nail holes,
a notebook and ghosts
lingering in the corners.

The Flexible Flyers that children
rode down white winter hills,
(rolling off to make snow angels at the bottom)
are left to sleep in the attic ...
but the snow angels come with us.

The piano has gone, but not the music we remember.
Chairs and china, tables and lamps, bookshelves and beds,
will find their way to other homes and other lives;
but our memories, light as thought,
packed into a space small as a heart,
are carried place to place on our intertwined hands.

This is a moving day;
the first day of the last of our lives.

The Last Page

The last page of the calendar has been turned
and a new year stretches out ahead.
Icy and brown now,
but with the promise of green meadows
and warm sun on the other side of March.

We have long sung together in the place
where time is measured not on a watch
ticking away hours
or a calendar ticking away years,
but by trying and failing and trying again,
accumulating layer by layer,
the geologic record of a lifetime.

Though we are old and our voices are weak;
though we may no longer remember the lyrics,
we will still hum the harmonies
of our long winter duet.

Time Passages

The Appointment in Samarra
(as retold by W. Somerset Maugham [1933])

The speaker is Death

There was a merchant in Bagdad who sent his servant to market to buy provisions and in a little while the servant came back, white and trembling, and said, "Master, just now when I was in the marketplace I was jostled by a woman in the crowd and when I turned I saw it was Death that jostled me. She looked at me and made a threatening gesture. Lend me your horse, and I will ride away from this city and avoid my fate. I will go to Samarra and there Death will not find me."

The merchant lent him his horse, and as fast as the horse could gallop, he went. Then the merchant went down to the marketplace and he saw me standing in the crowd and he came to me and said, "Why did you make a threatening gesture to my servant when you saw him this morning?"

"That was not a threatening gesture," I said," it was only a start of surprise. I was astonished to see him in Bagdad, for I had an appointment with him tonight in Samarra."

Before and After

The day began with coffee,
cream and sugar in a white china cup
painted with pink flowers.
The dogs stirred, circling my legs,
 mimicking the motion of my spoon.
Wind chimes called me to the porch,
to sit and watch an airplane
painting white contrails on a blue canvas of sky,
flying to catch up with tomorrow,
while I am rooted here.

The moon fell and the sun rose in a late September dance
set to the music of whispering trees and mockingbirds.
Distracted by the slow awakening
of my sleepy New England town,
it was nearly an hour
before the memories of mornings spent together
crept up silently to sit by my side.

Samarra

You can try to change the future;
you can rearrange the past.
You can argue for an option
but you cannot make it last.
The heart can have its reasons,
which reason cannot know
while all around you,
the winds of heaven blow.

No secrets still in hiding,
there's nothing left to show.
It's far too late for questions
and the answers come too slow.
You can feel the river flowing
but you can't tell where it goes
and you cannot know what's waiting
when the winds of heaven blow.

A beggar dressed in ragged clothes
points an empty sleeve
and asks if you can understand
the tapestry you weave.
There's a doorway you can't enter,
a door that you can't close
and all around you,
the winds of heaven blow.

Stand by one another
through the laughter and the tears.
Dance with one another
in the shadow of the years,
when the sound of the wind
is all you hear.

Caught In Between

In the wasteland
between Sunday noon and Monday morning,
I stand, photograph-still, on a beach
watching the sun burn a hole in the sky,
silvering the wings of the gulls
sandwiched between Wonder Bread clouds
and the watered-silk Pacific.

I am caught in between
an unremembered beginning
and an unforeseen end,
trapped inside the frame of a landscape
painted by a stranger's hand,
fading like a wedding-day rose
pressed between the pages of a book.

City Boy

Sleep won't come,
surrounded by the country quiet
rasping against my closed eyelids.
The hush that comforts philosophers and poets
feels to me like drowning in a sea of silence.

Let me hear the predatory growl of buses,
a car radio turned up too loud
or the whine of a motorcycle
revving up to its redline.
These are the sounds of people
awake and adventurous,
feeling the onshore breeze rise and fall,
swirling it around in their mouths like old Scotch,
tasting the salt and smoke from the beach,
reassuring me that out there,
beyond my window,
life is rushing like rainwater
through the streets.

Time Passages

A Small Sidewalk Café

The kids are all grown;
they have lives of their own.
Six years last winter my wife passed away.

I can't really say why I'm here in Marseilles,
watching the world from a small sidewalk café
where the old men play checkers until it gets dark.

Lovers hold hands as they walk through the park,
and I sit in the sunshine letting time drift away,
watching the street scene as April slips into May.

Oh, the women are fine, and their smiles are like wine
that goes straight to my head and my heart.
They're watching for friends who they're waiting to meet;
It makes me wish someone was waiting for me.

She sits at the same corner table each day,
writing a letter or reading a play.
When she stands up to leave, she glances my way
and I smile ... and search for something to say.

The end of the day comes and I'm still alone,
I can't help thinking it's time to go home.
But a sliver of moon's hanging over the bay,
so I linger awhile as the waiters stack up their trays.

Still the old men play checkers and talk of the girls
who they loved in their young yesterdays.
And I remember how I loved Renee
watching the world from a small sidewalk café.

Creation

The dogs swim silent circles in the lake
while I stand looking inward,
listening to the wind
whisper secrets in my ear.
An idea struggles from its shell,
pauses for a moment at the water's edge,
testing its wings, then takes a first uncertain
leap into the air, upward
through the morning fog.

Poetry is planets and stars;
words, floating like cosmic dust,
drawn together by some creative gravity.

Constellations

The curtain of clouds is lifting
on the stage of the evening sky.
The stars are weary,
cast in their unchanging roles
night after night until time itself ends.

Yet, without applause or bouquets of flowers,
the constellations play out their cosmic tragedy,
chasing around and around the nighttime set
like riders on a slow-spinning carousel,
pursuing and pursued,
but always just out of reach.

Silence

In spring, you finished my sentences
and sometimes my thoughts.
I could translate your sighs and sly asides,
paragraphs punctuated with pursed lips,
a hitched eyebrow or a lock of hair
twirled around your finger.
The lover's code that unlocked our doors.

But now, winter silence is your language,
an icy enigma I cannot decipher;
a threshold I cannot cross.
It's far too late to talk
about the thing that we both know.
It's time to let love go.

Confession

I have kept the secret in my heart long enough.
Naked, in a white tiled and curtained confessional,
the truth spills out of me
like the water that rains down from above;
a baptism to wash away my unoriginal sin.
I whisper to the walls,
and my words are reflected back,
'I don't love you anymore.'
For God's sake, don't ask why.
I can't explain it, not even to myself.

I've known I would need to tell you
but could not find the courage,
knowing if I said the words,
we would be frozen by them,
trapped in icy silence
at the moment of confession.

Dripping with doubt.
I stand before the mirror and stare,
searching in my eyes for absolution,
then wrap myself in a robe
and walk slowly,
over shards of broken promises,
toward the bedroom and the breaking day.
I think it's time to wake you now.

Just Close the Door

Your mind is made up,
your bags are all packed;
you're not coming back anymore.
You've explained all the whys
and said your goodbyes,
now all you have to do is just close the door.

It's time you learned that tables are for turning,
seasons for changing and bridges for burning.

The choices you make, make the life that you lead;
you give what you can and keep what you need.
You've spent all the time that you have to spend;
you've seen things through to the end,
now just close the door.

Closing doors is the hardest part.
Closing doors takes a change of heart.
You feel it to the core when you start closing doors.

Chris

I stuffed what was left of you
into a black plastic trash bag,
carried it out to the curb,
came back inside, and
exhausted, climbed into bed.

I awoke early
to the sound of grinding gears
and peeked out of the window
in time to see the bag
tossed into the trash masher and driven off.

Washed by relief, I wondered -
Now that the photographs,
saved birthday cards
and your battered fedora are gone,
will I finally be free of you?

Loose Change

You found me like loose change
discovered at the bottom
of a second-hand-store purse.
I was worn down, nicked at the edges,
tarnished – not worth a dollar.
But you cleaned me off,
shined me up
and put me in your pocket for safekeeping.

How long will it be
until I'm spent again,
passed from hand to hand
or left lying in the street?

I am afraid of the question,
afraid of the answer
and uncertain how to live in the in-between.

Edge of Love

Standing at the edge of love,
remembering the last time I fell.
Like a penny,
copper-bright and new
dropped into a wishing well.
Spinning down,
without a sound,
until I hit bottom
and my heart broke.

I never thought
I'd ever be standing here again,
waiting for a slow dance
to take another chance on love.

I only wish there was a fortune-teller
who could see if you would catch me
if I fall.

Reverie [An American Cinquain]

In dreams
she frees herself
from hands that cannot reach
and restless eyes that search for her
lost love.

Outgoing Tide

Water, tethered to the moon
like a dog on a leash
feeling its pull,
runs out of Perry's Mill pond,
exposing the mud bottom littered
with broken bottles,
algae-green rock and maimed toys.

When *our* calm and sparkling surface
is pulled away by life's centrifugal whirl,
uncovering discarded dreams,
moldering hopes
and lost opportunities,
all we can do
is wait for a kinder moon
to bring back concealing water
to soothe our wounds.

Writing Dance

Drops of blue-black ink,
like rain from some alien sky,
fall from my pen onto sheets of snow-white paper.
Letters ... words ... sentences bloom there
as if they were flowers in spring.
Ideas, drawn in lines and loops,
commas and quotation marks.
A minuet of mind and hand
which has been danced for ten thousand years.

We write for the same reason we sing -
to testify that we reached for heaven,
and though we could not catch hold of the wings of angels,
we managed to pluck a feather as they passed.

The Morning Crept Up

The morning crept up on me;
I didn't hear it coming.
It announced itself not with a shriek of sunlight,
but with the soft clatter of a neighbor's lawnmower
and the sound of children playing hide and seek.
It was Saturday,
summer,
and I was eleven.

There was a patch of sunlight
curled up on the bed next to me
as if it were a cat
and I could see a patch of blue just below the roofline,
like a lake stitched into a cloudy sky.

I heard the coffeepot percolating in the kitchen
and the popping of bacon frying
and my mother,
humming along with the radio.

Sabbath

I'm going away today...
just me and a six-string guitar,
packed into a scarred hard-shell case.

I won't be going far -
only out to the front porch.

I'll leave behind the morning traffic,
endless afternoons
and the evening news
and trade it for the feel of my fingers
moving over steel strings.

It will be a Sabbath -
a time when I stop trying to change the world.

Somewhere up Ahead

Driving through the night in this old car,
scratched and dented,
pitted by rusting regrets.
Dim headlights no longer
chase away the darkness.
Worn tires seem to find
every pothole of doubt and loss.

Long ago, there was a time
I drove with unfettered confidence,
even recklessness. A breakneck
rush to see, hear, feel
whatever the passing miles would bring.
Top down, sun on my face,
money in my pocket.
One hand draped over the wheel,
the other reaching for tomorrow.

But these days, I am a careful driver,
reading the signs,
staying between the lines.
Still following the road where it leads
but no longer in such a hurry
to reach the dark city
somewhere up ahead.

By(e) Chance

You were never good at waiting;
impatient from the day you arrived.
On the beach or in the woods,
you always ran ahead
as if you couldn't wait
to leave me behind.
But I could see you,
looking over your shoulder
or waiting around a bend
to be sure I was close by.
Then, reassured,
you were off again.

This time I can't follow
where you are going.
There is no bridge we can cross together,
but there is a path
that will lead you on from here.

You need to take it,
and I need to let you go.

Downsized

Downsized.
Rightsized.
Outsized.
Out of luck.
Out of time.
A pink-slipped, blue-collar worker
in a world that does not care
for old and well-worn clothes.

I am wrinkled and creased,
like an an outdated policy that,
having been read,
is stuffed into a file marked "History".

So, I hang in the closet ...
an out-of- style suit,
waiting for a day
when I will be taken down from the rack,
and pressed into service again.

A day when I will fit.

Kitchen Table

Once, the kitchen table was set for four.

Lauren was to the first to leave –
off to college in Ohio.
Then her younger brother Bill —
sometimes Liam or Will, but never Billy — left for Ramallah.
Seven months later, two Marines sat in the kitchen
and told us Bill wouldn't be coming home.
The year after that, it was you.
The city, the house and I
were too present reminders of the past
and the future that might have been.

These days, the table is set for one,
and it doesn't matter what's on my plate.

Go Out and Play

My brother, in a crouched stance,
waits on the cracked asphalt playground,
oil-darkened outfielder's glove resting on his knee.
I swing the Sears - Roebuck bat,
handle wrapped with tape,
hitting our worn ball into imagined bleachers
beyond his outstretched hand.

Those things are gone now.
The glove, decades ago, collected as trash.
The ball lost in the weeds,
or chewed into toy heaven by a dog.
The playground is now a parking lot;
my brother, a memory,
a name inscribed on a black marble monument.

What remains is the illusion
that sometimes comes on a summer morning.
I am twelve years old again,
hearing my mother call from the kitchen
"Go out and play...
and take your brother with you."

I wish I could.

So Close to Home

I set out on an ocean
of my own uncertainties.
Carried on the changing tides
I sailed just where I pleased.
I've felt the gentle southern breeze
and weathered northern storms.
My face got lined from searching
and my hands and heart got worn.

Packing all of my tomorrows
I left my home along the coast,
searching for the things
I thought I wanted most.
My sails were filled with winds of change;
I sailed out by the stars;
kept my eyes on the horizon,
which always seemed so far.

It's been a long, long journey
while I sat tending the flame.
It gave me time to wonder what's been lost
and what's been gained.
After years of watchful waiting,
trying to understand,
it's finally time to rest a while
here, in sight of land.

After all these years of wandering,
weary to the bone,
it seems so strange, so late in life,
to be so close to home.

If I Had Known

If I had known, I would have walked more slowly.

I could have watched the dogs chase each other
across the sand and water, like wolves at play
– or children.

I might have listened to how artfully
the symphony of the day was arranged,
not for horns and strings, but for woodpecker percussion,
a wind chime choir and the muted drone of traffic.

I'd have sat on the rough wooden bench by the seawall,
while the wind turned up the hood of my coat
like the ruffled collar of an aging king,
giving audience to his shell-subjects
and nodding at the applause of the waves.

I would have stayed longer –
until the light faded away
and the moon rose over the horizon
like the beacon of a distant lighthouse.

But instead, I walked quickly,
head down,
counting my steps by 50s,
impatient to get back,
because I didn't know.

Last Leaf

```
              The last
                    dying leaf
           shivers and twists        on the winter branch,
           attached to life            by a tenuous,
                  weathered stem                   holding
                              fast
                   even though                   it is now
             brown and brittle           the brilliance of its
                    autumn
                                    only a memory.

                      Let me,
                      one day,
                      go with
                      the gentle
                      grace of
                      leaves that
                      sought refuge
                      from cold,
                      battering winds,
             surrendering in an unrepentant
                      fall to the welcoming
                                  arms of the earth.
```

Time Passages

Old Man

The application for the Assisted Living facility had spaces, waiting for his Xs to move in.

Marital status: Single __ Married __ Widow(ed) _X_ Divorced __

Living alone?   Yes _X_   No ___

Friends/family nearby?   Yes __   No _X_

Interests: SCRABBLE on Wednesdays (with a neighbor's boy)

He's decided
not to play this crazy game anymore.
The Colt Viper is curled in his right hand
and a fat-neck bottle of wine in his left.
Not much remains.

The SCRABBLE game is miss ng lette s an way.

G me ov r

Biographical note

Paul Bluestein is a physician (done practicing), a blues guitar player (still practicing) and a dedicated Scrabble player (yes, ZAX is a word). He was born and raised in Philadelphia but has also lived in the Midwest and southern California. He currently lives in Connecticut with his wife and the two dogs that rescued him. He is fortunate to live near a lake which provides him a quiet place to think about the past, wonder about the future and lose his sunglasses.

www.ingramcontent.com/pod-product-compliance
Lightning Source LLC
Chambersburg PA
CBHW062150100526
44589CB00014B/1773